Color Ups of Illinois

The Grown Up Coloring Book

ISBN: 1516826701
ISBN-13: 978-1516826704

TO YOU

This book is dedicated to all those who had trouble staying in the lines as a child and want a do over.

Color Ups are a photographic rendering in coloring book format, specifically designed for Grown Ups.

Ilinois Trivia Facts

Walt Disney was born in Chicago.

The world's longest street is in Chicago - Western Ave.

The world's largest gum manufacturer is in Chicago - William Wrigley.

The world's first Ferris Wheel was at the Columbian Exposition in Chicago.

The first aquarium opened in Chicago.

Chicago is know as the "Candy Capital of the World".

The Chicago River is the only river in the world that flows backwards.

McCormick Place in Chicago has the largest amount of exhibit space for a convention center in the U.S.

Metropolis - the home of Superman is in Southern Illinois.

The world's largest ice cream cone factory is located in Chicago - Keebler.

The Twinkie was invented in Chicago.

Dixon is the home of Ronald Regan.

Illinois was the first to ratify the 13th Amendment - abolishing slavery.

Harrison Ford is a native Chicagoan.

Miracle on 34th Street was filmed in Chicago.

Roller skates, spray paint and pinball games were invented in Chicago.

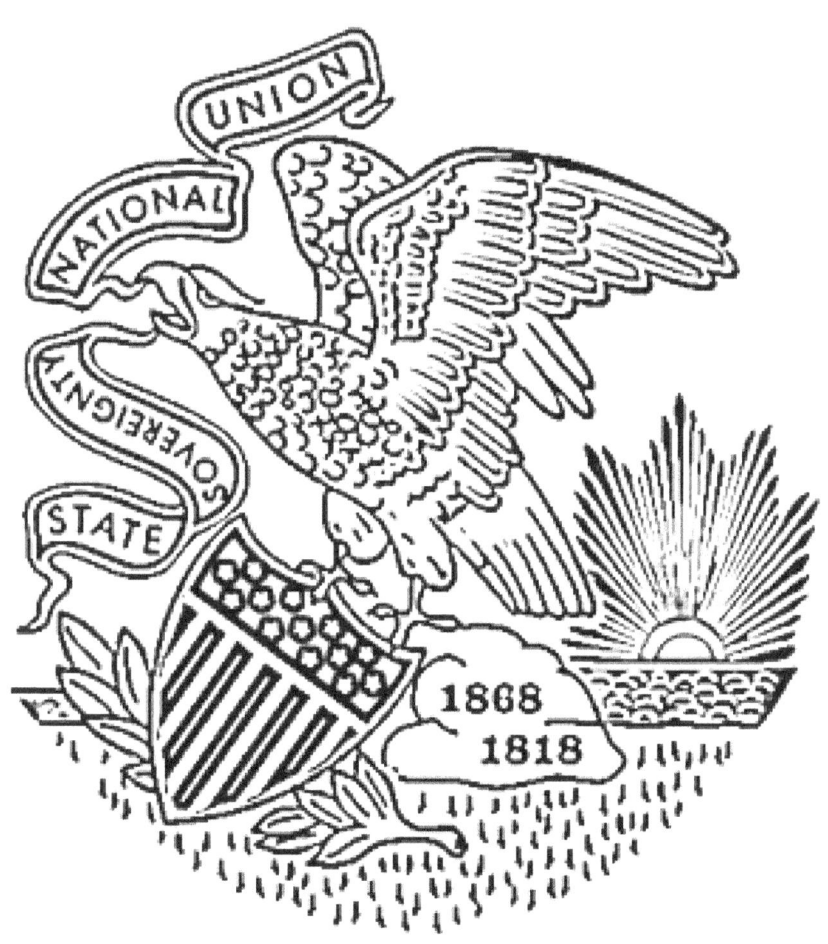

ILLINOIS

The Chicago Skyline

Chicago is located in northeastern Illinois on the southwestern shores of Lake Michigan. It is the principal city in the Chicago Metropolitan Area situated in the Midwestern United States and the Great Lakes region. Chicago rests on a continental divide at the site of the Chicago Portage, connecting the Mississippi River and the Great Lakes watersheds. The city lies beside huge freshwater Lake Michigan, and two rivers—The Chicago River in downtown and the Calumet River in the industrial far South Side—flow entirely or partially through Chicago. Chicago's history and economy are closely tied to its proximity to Lake Michigan. While the Chicago River historically handled much of the region's waterborne cargo, today's huge lake freighters use the city's Lake Calumet Harbor on the South Side. The lake also provides another positive effect, moderating Chicago's climate; making waterfront neighborhoods slightly warmer in winter and cooler in summer

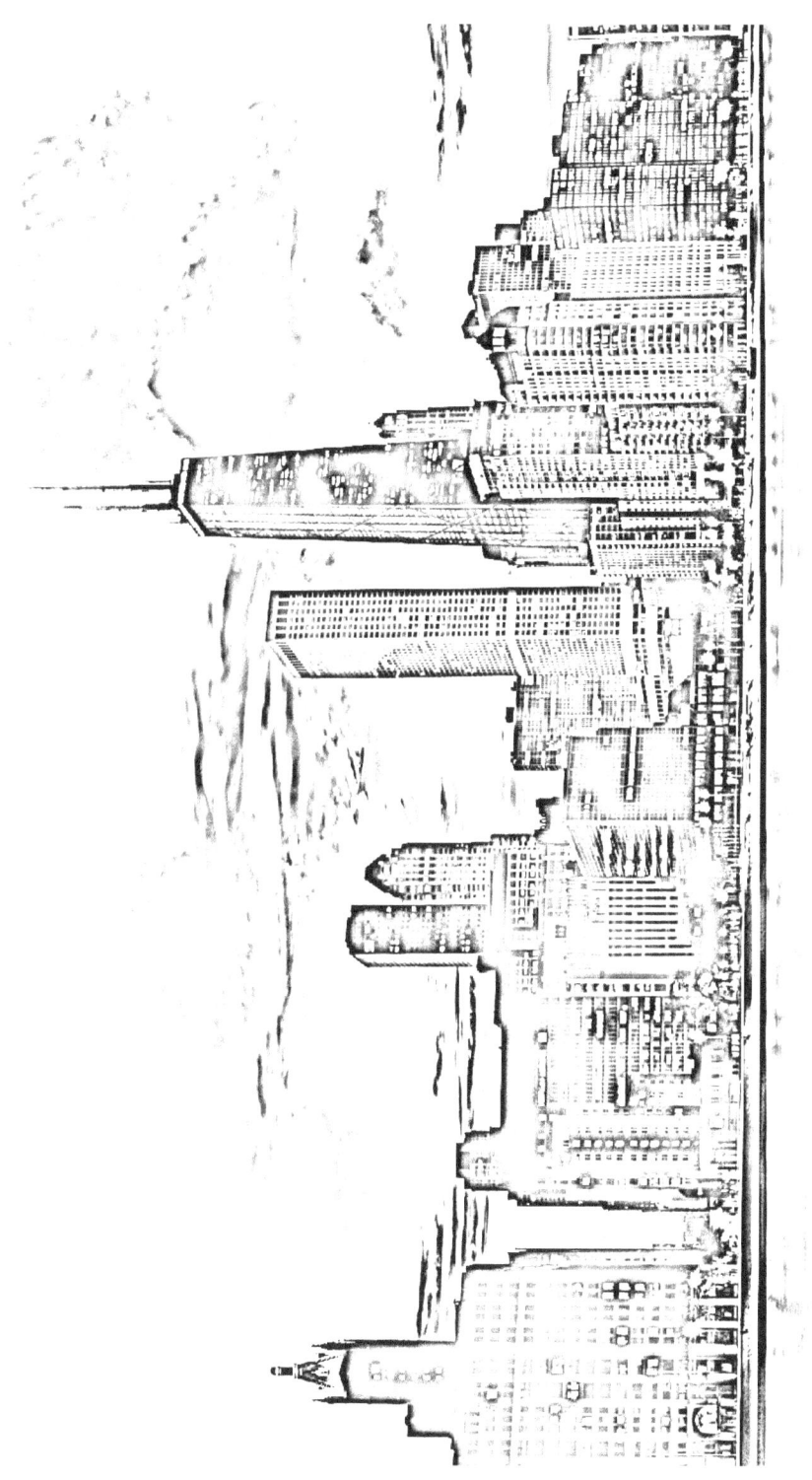

Wrigley Field

Wrigley Field is a baseball park located in the North Side district of Chicago, Illinois. It is the home of the Chicago Cubs, the city's Major League Baseball (MLB) franchise.

It was built in 1914 as Weeghman Park for the Chicago Federal League baseball team, the Chicago Whales. The Cubs played their first game at Weeghman Park on April 20, 1916, defeating the Cincinnati Reds 7–6 in eleven innings. In November 1918, Weeghman resigned as team president. Chewing gum magnate William Wrigley, Jr. acquired complete control of the Cubs by 1921. It was called Cubs Park from 1920 through 1926, before officially becoming Wrigley Field for the 1927 season.

Located in the north side community area of Lakeview, Wrigley Field sits on an irregular block bounded by Clark (west) and Addison (south) Streets and Waveland (north) and Sheffield (east) Avenues. Wrigley Field is nicknamed The Friendly Confines, a phrase popularized by "Mr. Cub", Hall of Famer Ernie Banks. The current seating capacity is 41,688. It is the oldest National League ballpark, the second-oldest active major league ballpark (after Fenway Park on April 20, 1912), and the only remaining Federal League park.

Wrigley Field is known for its ivy-covered brick outfield wall, the unusual wind patterns off Lake Michigan, the iconic red marquee over the main entrance, the hand-turned scoreboard, and for being the last major league park to have lights installed for play after dark, with lighting installed in 1988. The area surrounding the ballpark contains residential streets, in addition to bars, restaurants and other establishments, and is called Wrigleyville. Between 1921 and 1970, it was also the home of the Chicago Bears of the National Football League. It hosted the 2009 National Hockey League Winter Classic between the Chicago Blackhawks and the Detroit Red Wings, on January 1, 2009.

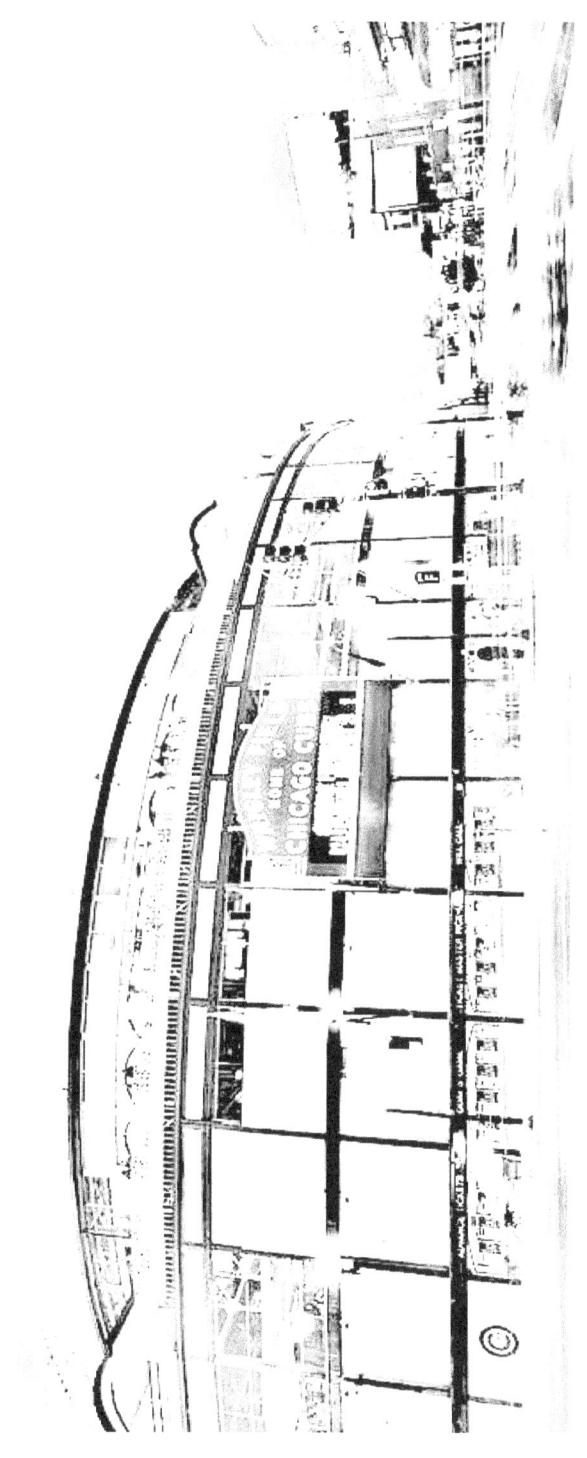

Comiskey Park

Comiskey Park was a ballpark in Chicago, Illinois, the home of the Chicago White Sox from 1910 through 1990. Built by owner Charles Comiskey and designed by Zachary Taylor Davis, it hosted four World Series and more than 6,000 Major League Baseball games. The field was also the site of the 1937 heavyweight title match in which Joe Louis defeated then champion James J. Braddock in eight rounds.

The Chicago Cardinals of the National Football League also called Comiskey Park home when they weren't playing at Normal Park or Soldier Field. The Cardinals won the 1947 NFL Championship Game over the Philadelphia Eagles at Comiskey Park.
A new ballpark opened in 1991, across 35th Street and south of its predecessor, and Comiskey Park was demolished the same year. Originally also called Comiskey Park, it was renamed U.S. Cellular Field in 2003.

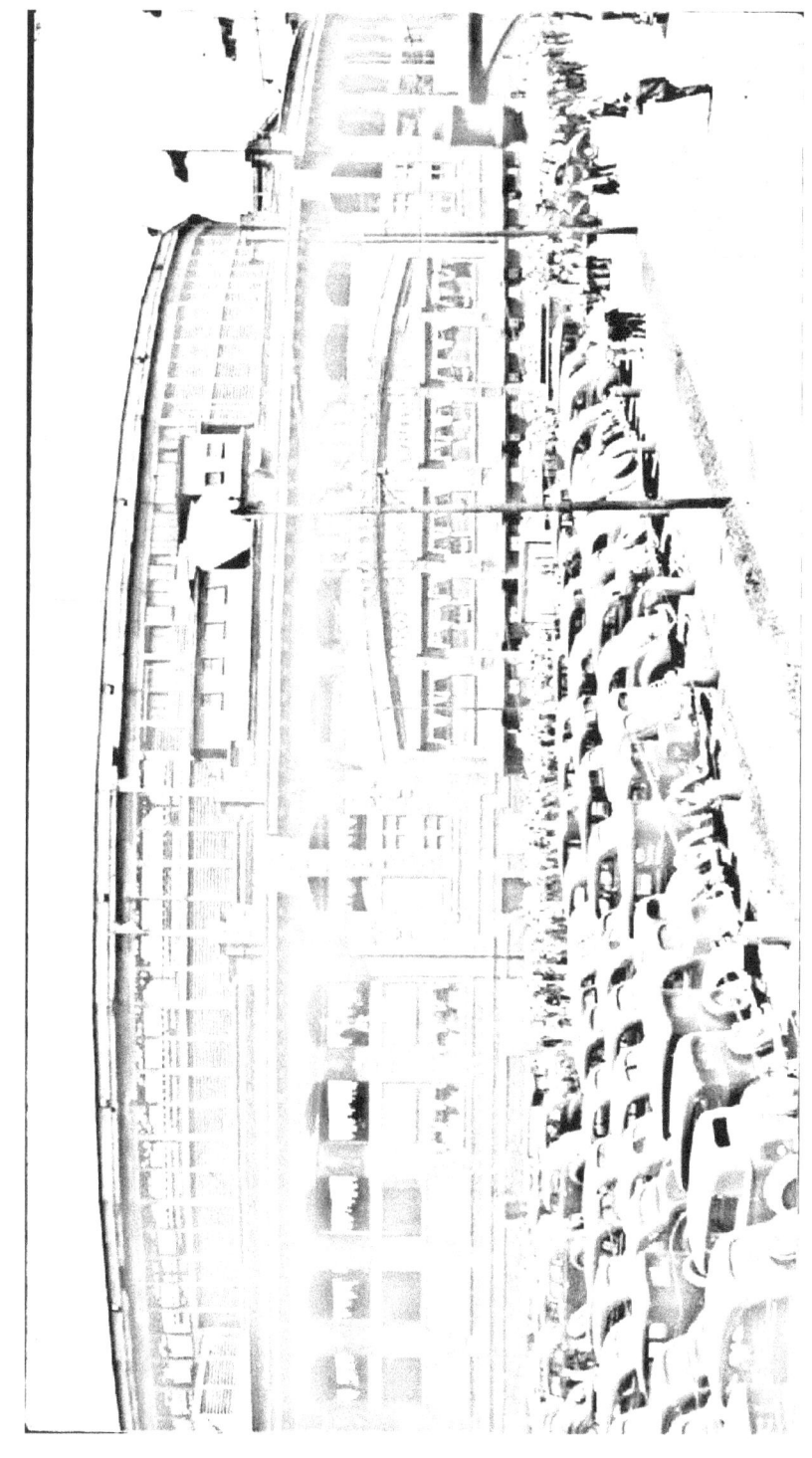

Soldier Field

Soldier Field is an American football stadium on the Near South Side of Chicago, Illinois, United States. Opened in 1924, it is the oldest NFL stadium, celebrating 90 years of operation. Since 1971 it has been the home of the National Football League's Chicago Bears. With a football capacity of 61,500, it is the third smallest stadium in the NFL. In 2003, the interior underwent extensive renovation.

The field serves as a memorial to American soldiers who have died in wars. It was designed in 1919 and opened on October 9, 1924, as Municipal Grant Park Stadium, changing its name to Soldier Field on November 11, 1925. It was named after winning a contest held by a Chicago newspaper. Edward Mueller was the winner. Originally the name plate was erected "Soldiers" field, but was corrected after Mueller wrote the paper back. Its formal dedication as Soldier Field was on Saturday, November 27, 1926, during the 29th annual playing of the Army–Navy Game. Its design is modeled on the Greco-Roman architectural tradition, with doric columns rising above the entrance.

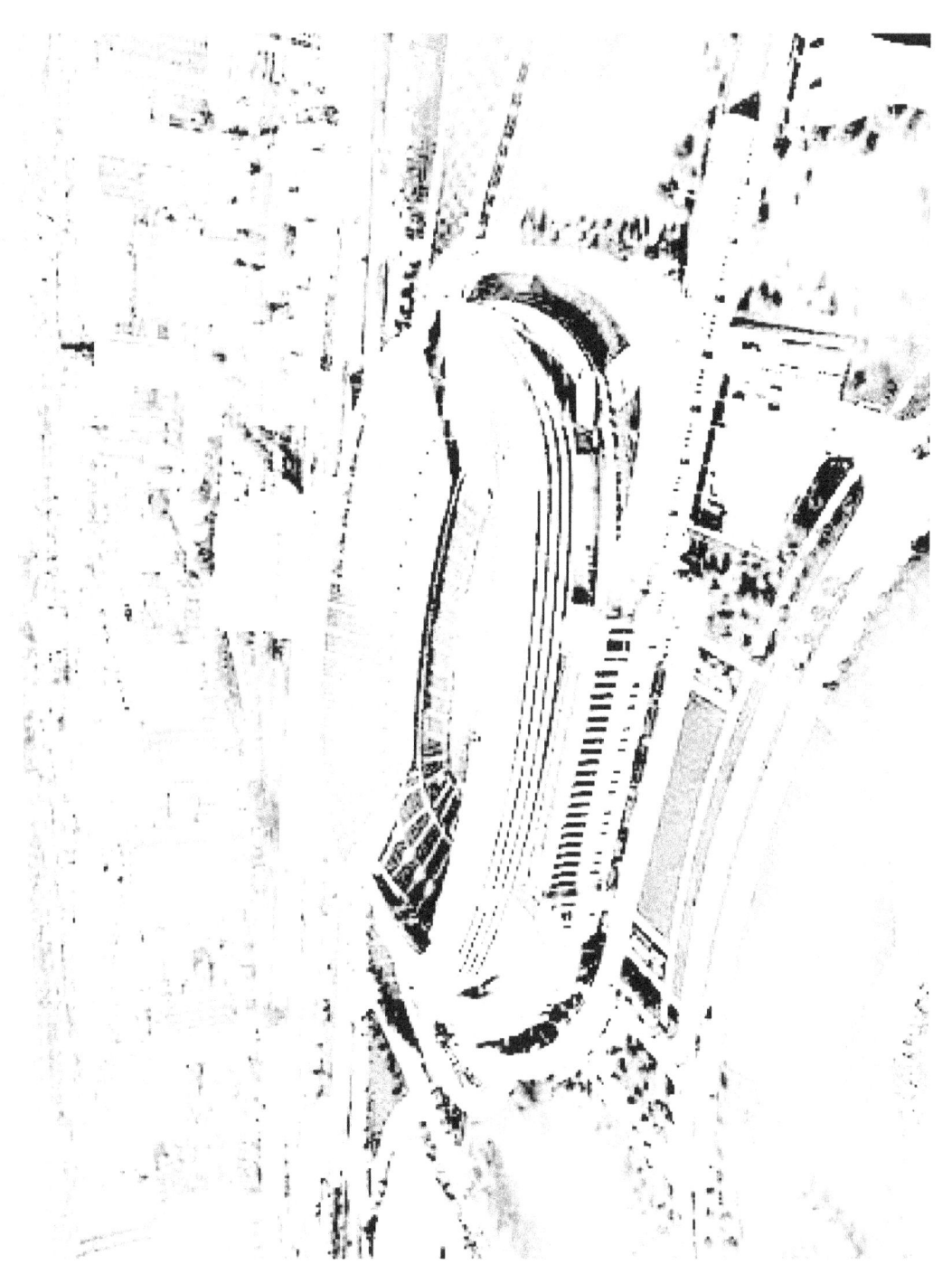

Field Museum

The Field Museum of Natural History, located in Chicago, Illinois, USA, is one of the largest natural history museums in the world. The museum maintains its status as a premier natural history museum through the size and quality of its educational and scientific programs, as well as due to its extensive scientific specimen and artifact collections. The diverse, high quality permanent exhibitions, which attract up to 2 million visitors annually, range from the earliest fossils to past and current cultures from around the world to interactive programming demonstrating today's urgent conservation needs.

Additionally, the Field Museum maintains a temporary exhibition program of traveling shows as well as in-house produced topical exhibitions. The professional staff maintains collections of over 24 million specimens and objects that provide the basis for the museum's scientific research programs. These collections include the full range of existing biodiversity, gems, meteorites, fossils, as well as rich anthropological collections and cultural artifacts from around the globe. The Field Museum Library, which contains over 275,000 books, journals, and photo archives focused on biological systematics, evolutionary biology, geology, archaeology, ethnology and material culture, supports the Field Museum's academic research faculty and exhibit development.

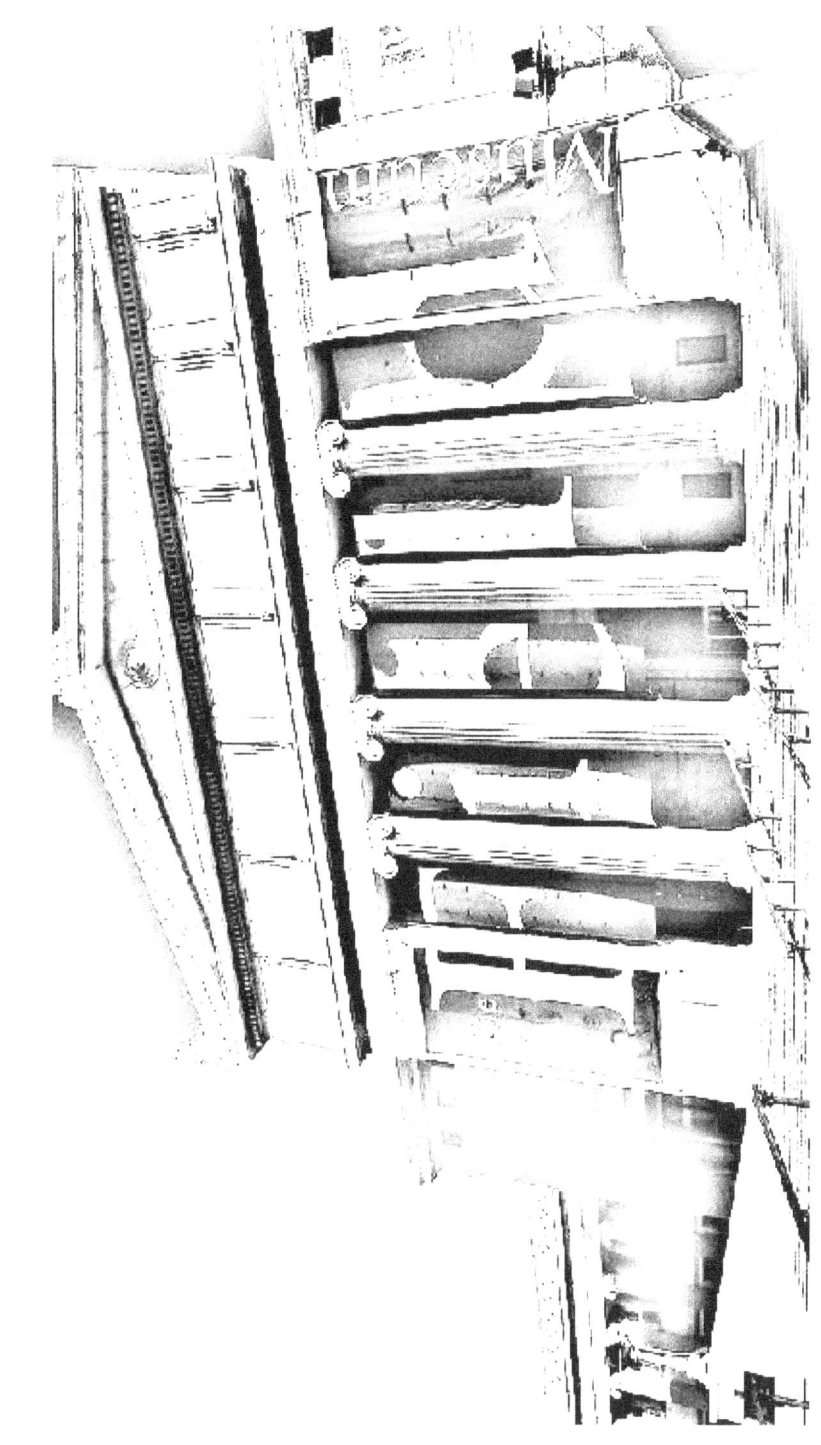

Sue The T-Rex

"Sue" is the nickname given to FMNH PR 2081, which is the largest, most extensive and best preserved Tyrannosaurus rex specimen ever found. It has a length of 12.9 metres (42 ft), stands 4 metres (13 ft) tall at the hips, and was estimated to have weighed more than 6.4 metric tons when alive. It was discovered in the summer of 1990 by Sue Hendrickson, a paleontologist, and was named after her. After ownership disputes were settled, the fossil was auctioned in October 1997 for US $7.6 million, the highest amount ever paid for a dinosaur fossil, and is now a permanent feature at the Field Museum of Natural History in Chicago, Illinois.

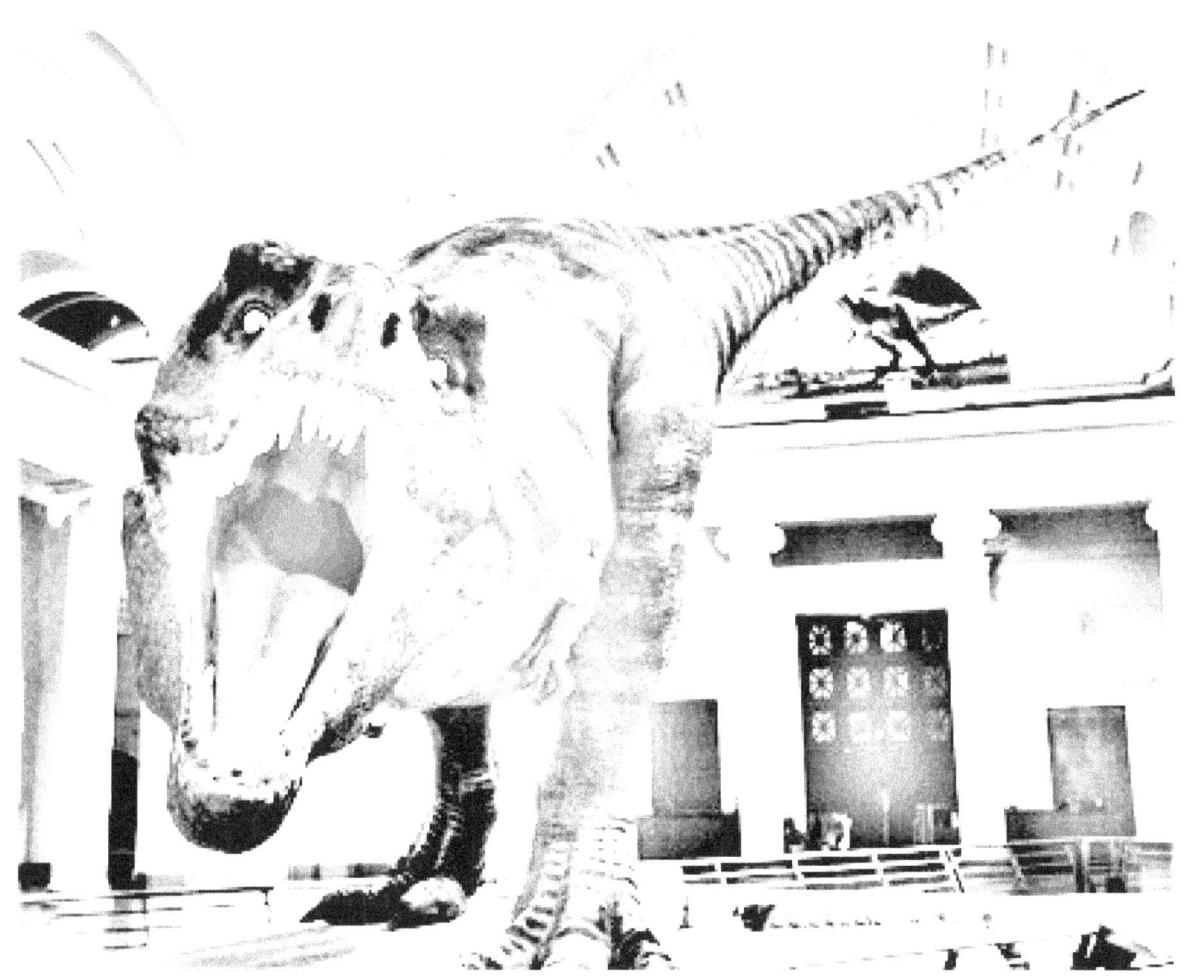

The Museum of Science and Industry

The Museum of Science and Industry (MSI) is located in Chicago, Illinois, in Jackson Park, in the Hyde Park neighborhood between Lake Michigan and The University of Chicago. It is housed in the former Palace of Fine Arts from the 1893 World's Columbian Exposition. Initially endowed by Julius Rosenwald, the Sears, Roebuck and Company president and philanthropist, it was supported by the Commercial Club of Chicago and opened in 1933 during the Century of Progress Exposition.

It is the largest science museum in the western hemisphere. Among its diverse and expansive exhibits, the museum features a full-size replica coal mine, a German submarine (U-505) captured during World War II, a 3,500-square-foot (330 m2) model railroad, the first diesel-powered streamlined stainless-steel passenger train (Pioneer Zephyr), and the Apollo 8 spacecraft that carried the first humans to orbit the Moon.

Based on 2009 attendance, the Museum of Science and Industry was the second largest cultural attraction in Chicago. David R. Mosena has been President and CEO of the Museum since 1998.

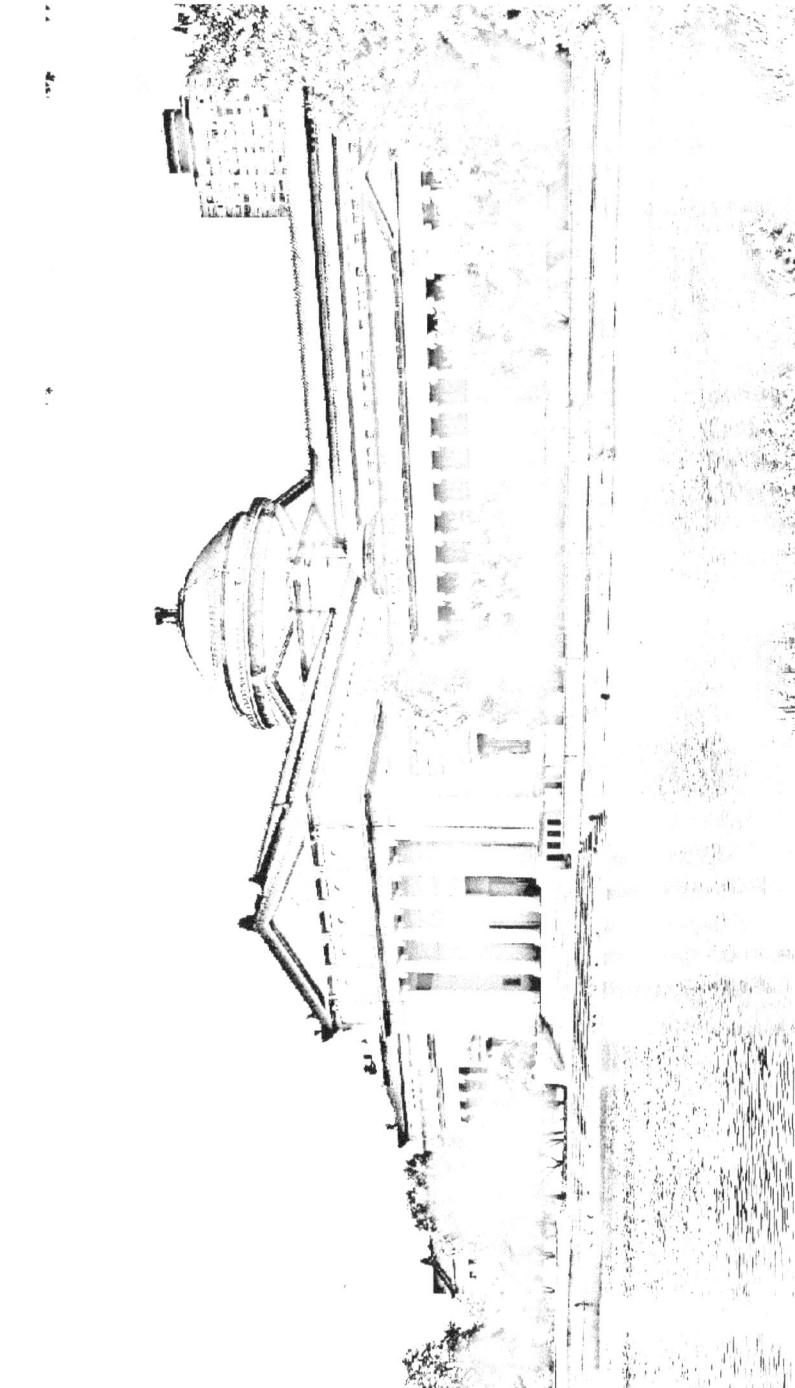

The Art Institute of Chicago

The Art Institute of Chicago (AIC) is an encyclopedic art museum located in Chicago's Grant Park. It features a collection of Impressionist and Post-Impressionist art in its permanent collection. Its holdings also include American art, Old Masters, European and American decorative arts, Asian art, modern and contemporary art, and architecture and industrial and graphic design. In addition, it houses the Ryerson & Burnham Libraries.

Tracing its history to a free art school and gallery founded in 1866, the museum is located at 111 South Michigan Avenue in the Chicago Landmark Historic Michigan Boulevard District. It is associated with the School of the Art Institute of Chicago and is overseen by Director and President Douglas Druick. It is one of the most visited art museums in the world with about 1.5 million visitors annually (2013), and with one million square feet in eight buildings, it is the second-largest art museum in the United States, after the Metropolitan Museum of Art.

One of the two lion statues (Kemeys, bronze 1893) flanking the Institute's main entrances.

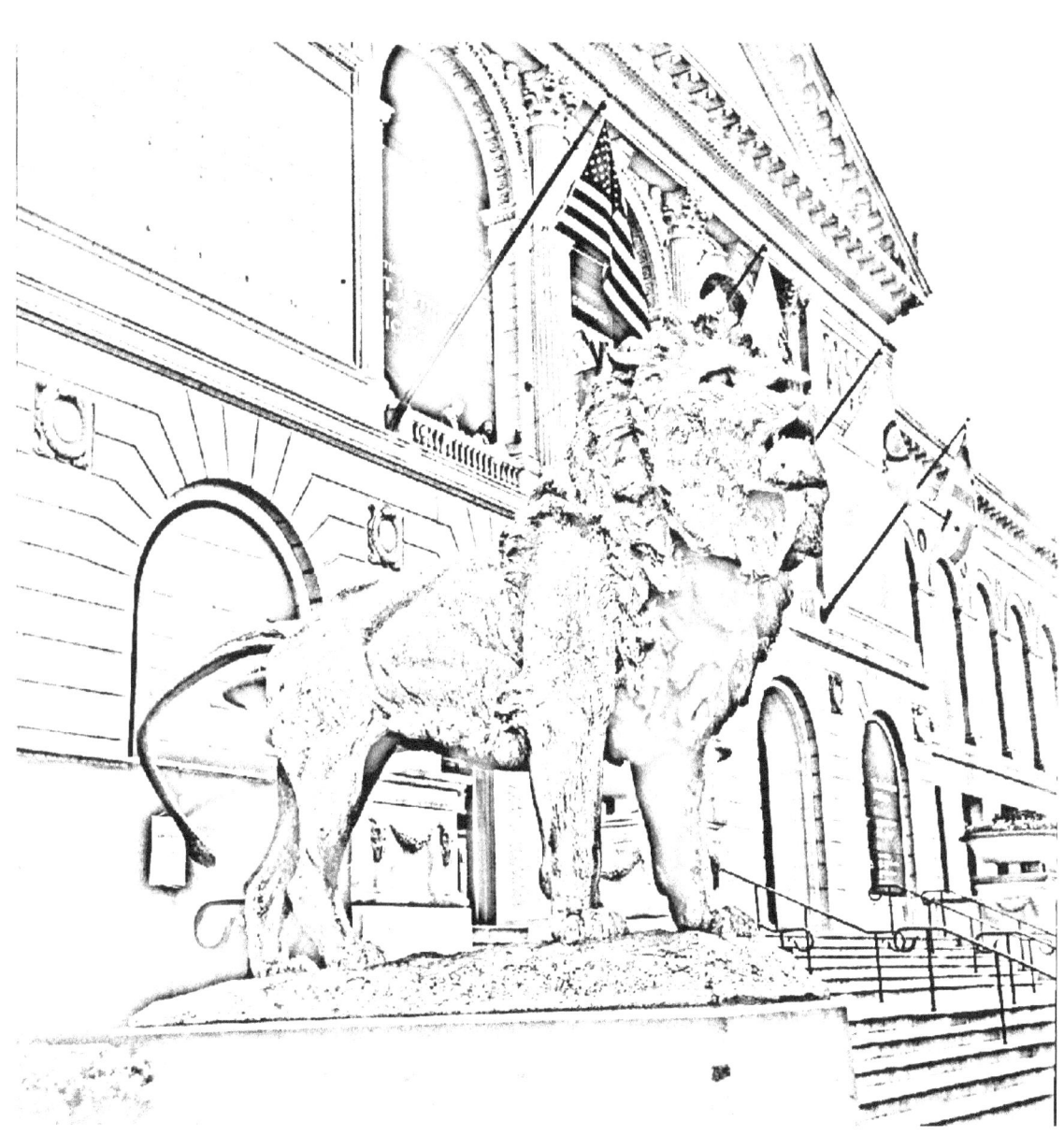

Abraham Lincoln Home in Springfield

Lincoln Home National Historic Site preserves the Springfield, Illinois home and a historic district where Abraham Lincoln lived from 1844 to 1861, before becoming the 16th President of the United States. The presidential memorial includes the four blocks surrounding the home and a visitor center.

The house, purchased by Lincoln and his wife, Mary Todd Lincoln in 1844, was the only home that Lincoln ever owned. Located at the corner of Eighth and Jackson Streets, the house contains twelve rooms spread over two floors. During the time he lived here, Lincoln was elected to the House of Representatives in 1846, and elected President in 1860.

Lincoln's son, Robert Todd Lincoln donated the family home to the State of Illinois in 1887 under the condition that it would forever be well-maintained and open to the public at no charge. The home and Lincoln Tomb, also in Springfield, were designated National Historic Landmarks on December 19, 1960, and automatically listed on the National Register of Historic Places on October 15, 1966. The home and adjacent district became a National Historic Site on August 18, 1971 and is owned and administered by the National Park Service. As of 2014, it is the only National Park Service property in Illinois.

Along with the Lincoln Home, several other structures within the four-block area are also preserved. All the homes have been restored to their appearance during the time Lincoln lived in the neighborhood. Two of these structures, the Dean House and the Arnold House, are open to visitors and house exhibits on the life and times of Lincoln and his neighbors. In total, the buildings included in the park occupy 12 acres (49,000 m2).

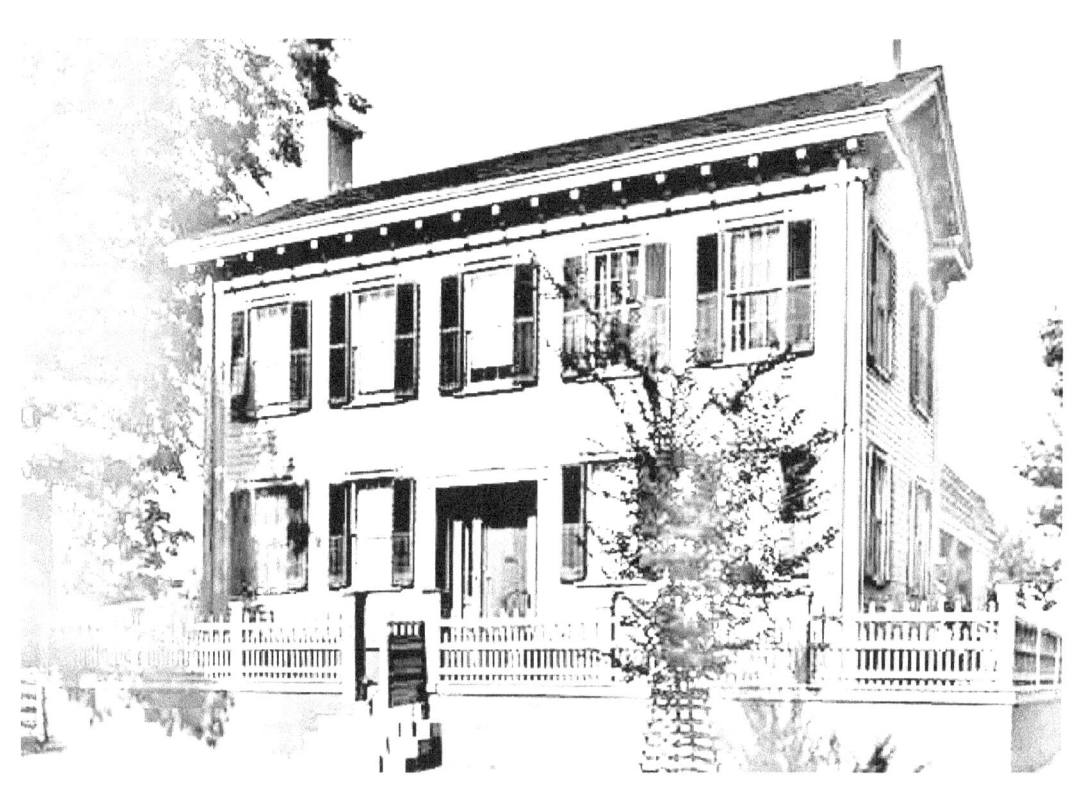

Cloud Gate (The Bean)

Cloud Gate is a public sculpture by Indian-born British artist Anish Kapoor, that is the centerpiece of AT&T Plaza at Millennium Park in the Loop community area of Chicago, Illinois. The sculpture and AT&T Plaza are located on top of Park Grill, between the Chase Promenade and McCormick Tribune Plaza & Ice Rink. Constructed between 2004 and 2006, the sculpture is nicknamed The Bean because of its shape. Made up of 168 stainless steel plates welded together, its highly polished exterior has no visible seams. It measures 33 by 66 by 42 feet (10 by 20 by 13 m), and weighs 110 short tons (100 t; 98 long tons).

Kapoor's design was inspired by liquid mercury and the sculpture's surface reflects and distorts the city's skyline. Visitors are able to walk around and under Cloud Gate's 12-foot (3.7 m) high arch. On the underside is the "omphalos" (Greek for "navel"), a concave chamber that warps and multiplies reflections. The sculpture builds upon many of Kapoor's artistic themes, and it is popular with tourists as a photo-taking opportunity for its unique reflective properties.
The sculpture was the result of a design competition. After Kapoor's design was chosen, numerous technological concerns regarding the design's construction and assembly arose, in addition to concerns regarding the sculpture's upkeep and maintenance. Various experts were consulted, some of whom believed the design could not be implemented. Eventually, a feasible method was found, but the sculpture's construction fell behind schedule. It was unveiled in an incomplete form during the Millennium Park grand opening celebration in 2004, before being concealed again while it was completed. Cloud Gate was formally dedicated on May 15, 2006, and has since gained considerable popularity, both domestically and internationally.

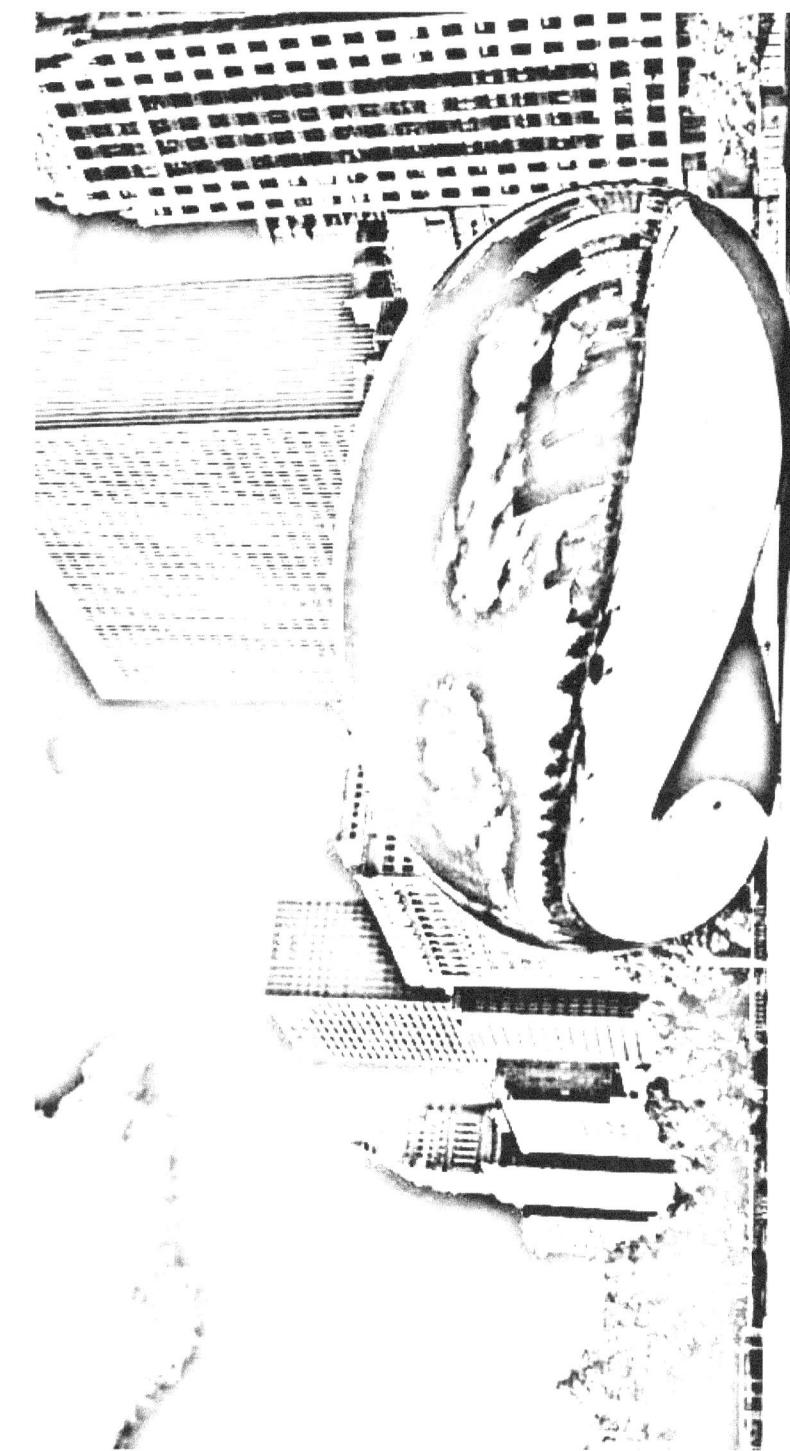

Buckingham Fountain

Buckingham Fountain is a Chicago landmark in the center of Grant Park. Dedicated in 1927, it is one of the largest fountains in the world. Built in a rococo wedding cake style and inspired by the Latona Fountain at the Palace of Versailles, it is meant to allegorically represent Lake Michigan. It operates from April to October, with regular water shows and evening color-light shows. During the winter, the fountain is decorated with festival lights.

The fountain is considered Chicago's front door, since it resides in Grant Park, the city's front yard near the intersection of Columbus Drive and Congress Parkway. The fountain itself represents Lake Michigan, with each sea horse symbolizing the states of Illinois, Wisconsin, Michigan and Indiana, that border the lake. The fountain was designed by beaux arts architect Edward H. Bennett. The statues were created by the French sculptor Marcel F. Loyau. The design of the fountain was inspired by the Bassin de Latome and modeled after Latona Fountain at Versailles.

> The fountain was donated to the city by Kate Buckingham in memory of her brother, Clarence Buckingham, and was constructed at a cost of $750,000. The fountain's official name is the Clarence Buckingham Memorial Fountain. Kate Buckingham also established the Buckingham Fountain Endowment Fund with an initial investment of $300,000 to pay for maintenance. Buckingham Fountain was dedicated on August 26, 1927.

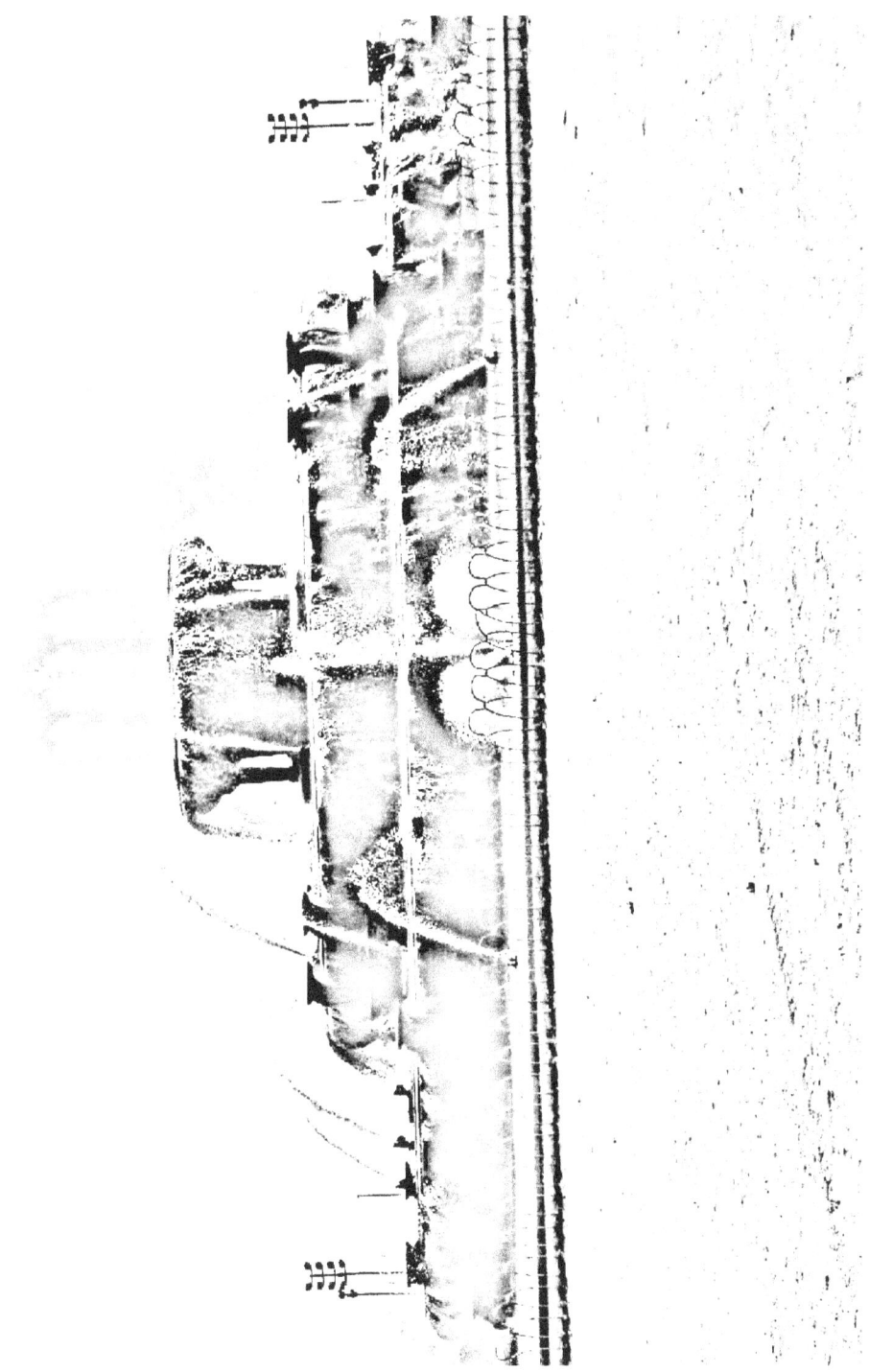

The Chicago River

The Chicago River is a system of rivers and canals with a combined length of 156 miles (251 km) that runs through the city of Chicago, including its center (the Chicago Loop). Though not especially long, the river is notable for being a reason why Chicago became an important location, with the related Chicago Portage being a link between the Great Lakes and the Mississippi Valley waterways and eventually the Gulf of Mexico.

The River is also noteworthy for its natural and man-made history. In 1887, the Illinois General Assembly, partly in response to concerns arising out of an extreme weather event in 1885 that threatened the city's water supply, decided to reverse the flow of the Chicago River through civil engineering by taking water from Lake Michigan and discharging it into the Mississippi River watershed. In 1889, the Illinois General Assembly created the Chicago Sanitary District (now The Metropolitan Water Reclamation District) to replace the Illinois-Michigan Canal, which had become inadequate to carry the city's increasing sewage and commercial navigation needs, with the Chicago Sanitary and Ship Canal, a much larger waterway. The District completed this man-made hydrologic connection between the Great Lakes and Mississippi watershed in 1900 by reversing the flow of the Main Stem and South Branch of the river using a series of canal locks, and increasing the river's flow from Lake Michigan, causing it to empty into the new Canal. In 1999, this system was named a 'Civil Engineering Monument of the Millennium' by the American Society of Civil Engineers (ASCE).

The river is memorialized, in part, by two horizontal blue stripes on the Municipal Flag of Chicago. The river also serves as inspiration for one of Chicago's ubiquitous symbols: a three-branched, Y-shaped symbol (called the municipal device) is found on many buildings and other structures throughout Chicago; it represents the three branches of the Chicago River.

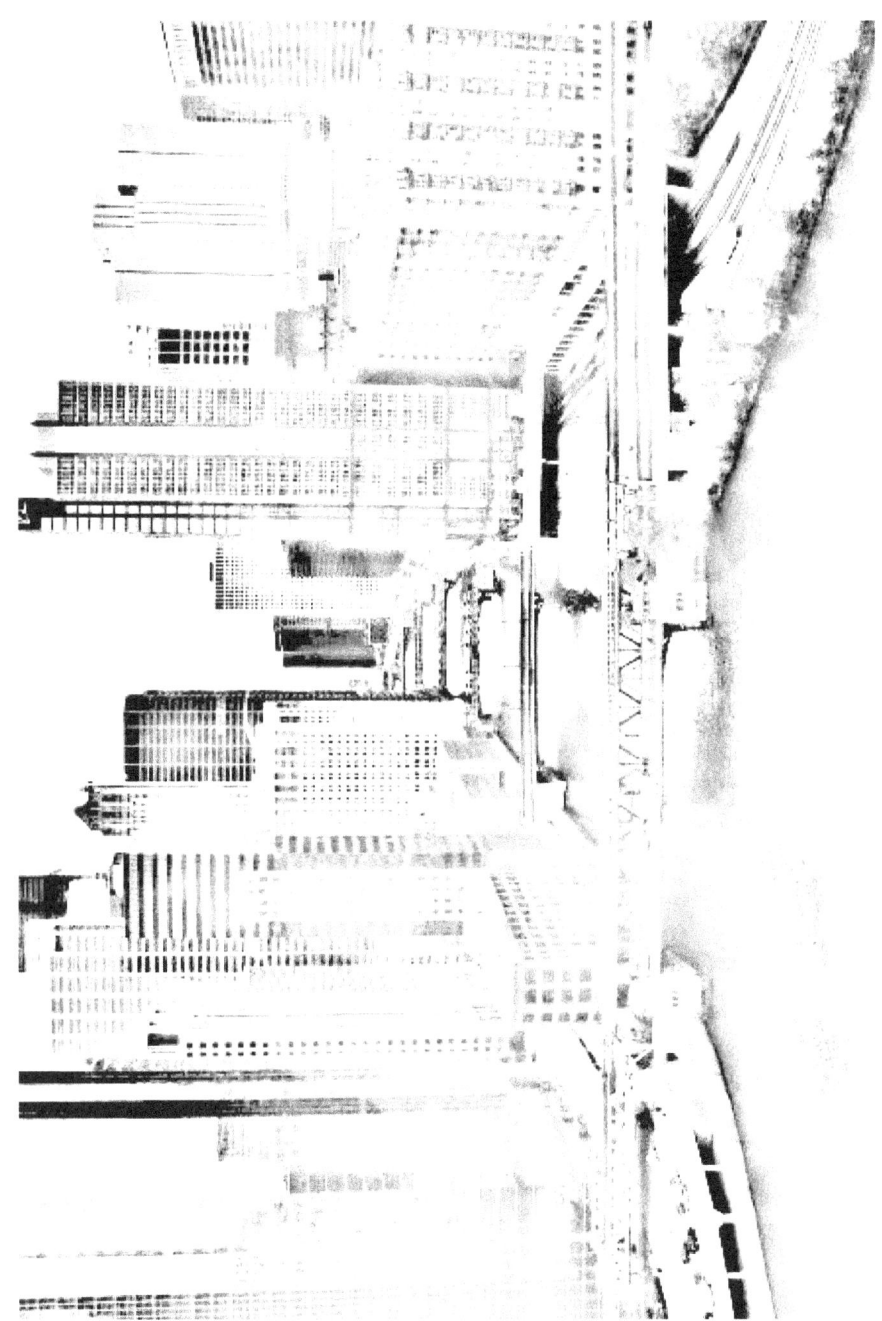

LINCOLN TOMB WAR MEMORIAL

Lincoln Tomb is the final resting place of the 16th President of the United States, Abraham Lincoln, his wife, Mary Todd Lincoln, and three of their four sons. It is located in Oak Ridge Cemetery in Springfield, Illinois. At the close of the events marking Lincoln's death, his body was placed in a nearby receiving tomb and later in the state tomb. The mausoleum is owned and administered by the State of Illinois as Lincoln Tomb State Historic Site. It was designated one of the first National Historic Landmarks in 1960, and thus became one of the first sites listed on the National Register of Historic Places in 1966, when that designation was created.

On April 15, 1865, the day President Lincoln died, a group of Springfield citizens formed the National Lincoln Monument Association and spearheaded a drive for funds to construct a memorial or tomb. Upon arrival of the funeral train on May 3, Lincoln lay in state in the Illinois State Capitol for one night. After the funeral the next day, his coffin was placed in a receiving vault at Oak Ridge Cemetery, the site Mrs. Lincoln requested for burial. In December, her husband's remains were removed to a temporary vault not far from the proposed memorial site. The location of the temporary vault is today marked with a small granite marker on the hill behind the current tomb. In 1871, three years after laborers had begun constructing the tomb, the body of Lincoln and those of the three youngest of his sons were placed in crypts in the unfinished structure.

In 1874, upon completion of the memorial, which had been designed by Larkin Goldsmith Mead, Lincoln's remains were interred in a marble sarcophagus in the center of a chamber known as the "catacombs," or burial room. In 1876, however, after two Chicago criminals failed in an attempt to steal Lincoln's body and hold it for ransom, the National Lincoln Monument Association hid it in another part of the memorial, first under wood and other debris and then buried in the ground within the tomb. When Mrs. Lincoln died in 1882, her remains were placed with those of Lincoln, but in 1887 both bodies were reburied in a brick vault beneath the floor of the burial room.

By 1895, the year the State acquired the memorial, it had fallen into disrepair. During a rebuilding and restoration program in 1899–1901, all five caskets were moved to a nearby subterranean vault. In the later year, State officials returned them to the burial room and placed that of Lincoln in the sarcophagus it had occupied in 1874–1876. Within a few months, however, at the request of Robert Todd Lincoln, the President's only surviving son, the body was moved to its final resting place, a concrete vault 10 feet (3.0 m) below the surface of the burial room.

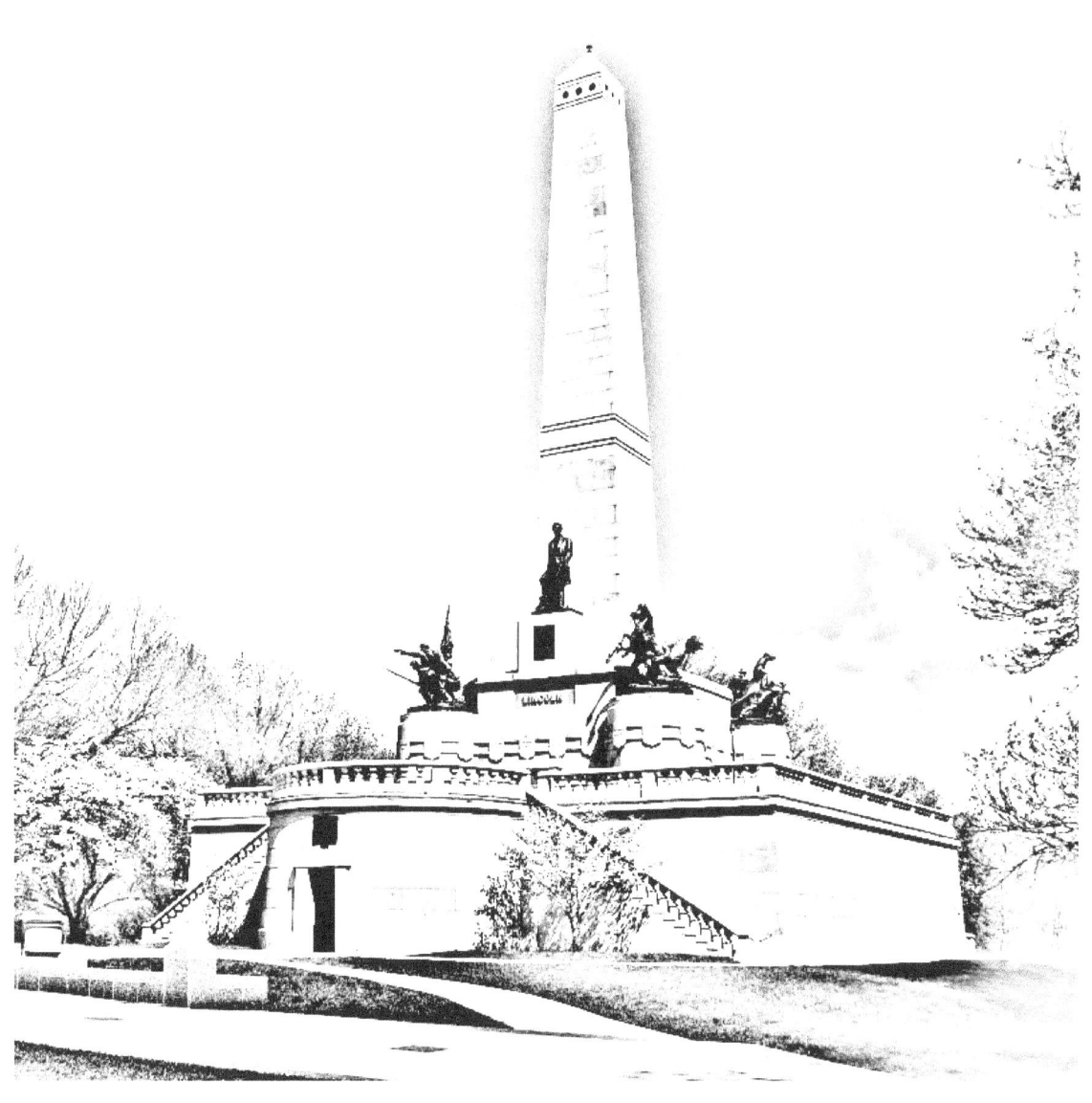

The Chicago L

The Chicago "L" (short for "elevated") is the rapid transit system serving the city of Chicago and some of its surrounding suburbs in the U.S. state of Illinois. It is operated by the Chicago Transit Authority (CTA). It is the fourth largest rapid transit system in the United States in terms of total route length (at 102.8 miles (165.4 km) long), and the third busiest rail mass transit system in the United States after the Washington Metro. Chicago's "L" provides 24-hour service on some portions of its network, being one of only four heavy rail rapid transit systems in the United States (the "L", New York City Subway, PATH, and Philadelphia's PATCO Speed line) to do so. The oldest sections of the "L" started operations in 1892, making it the second-oldest rapid transit system in the Americas, after Boston's "T". The "L" has been credited with fostering the growth of Chicago's dense city core that is one of the city's distinguishing features. The "L" consists of eight rapid transit lines laid out in a spoke-hub distribution paradigm mainly focusing transit towards the Loop. Although the "L" gained its nickname because large parts of the system are elevated, portions of the network are also in subway tunnels, at grade level, or open cut.

In 2013, the "L" had an average of 726,459 passenger boarding's each weekday, 456,993 each Saturday, and 328,553 each Sunday. In a 2005 poll, Chicago Tribune readers voted it one of the "seven wonders of Chicago," behind the lakefront and Wrigley Field but ahead of Willis Tower (formerly the Sears Tower), the Water Tower, the University of Chicago, and the Museum of Science and Industry.

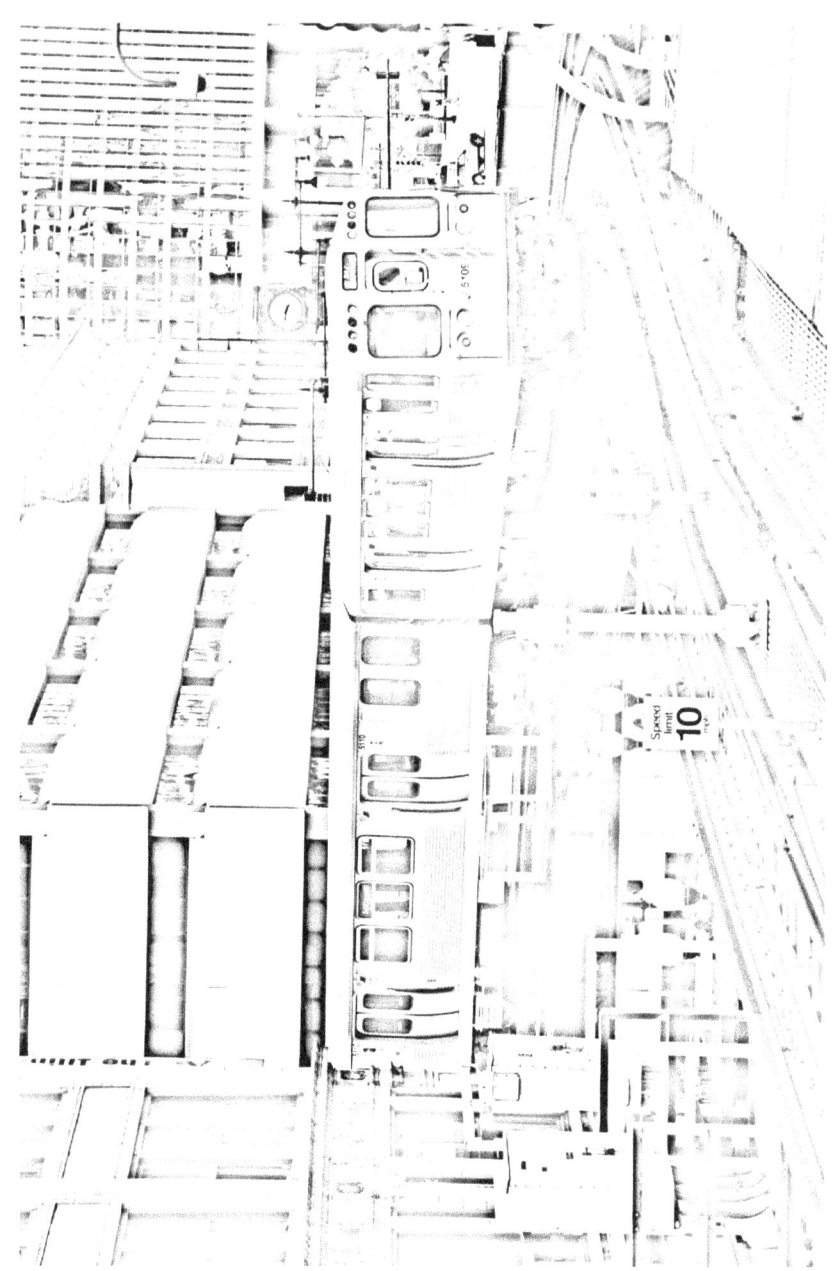

Navy Pier

Navy Pier is a 3,300-foot-long (1,010 m) pier on the Chicago shoreline of Lake Michigan. It is located in the Streeterville neighborhood of the Near North Side community area. The pier was built in 1916 at a cost of $4.5 million. It was a part of the Plan of Chicago developed by architect and city planner Daniel Burnham and his associates. As Municipal Pier #2 (Municipal Pier #1 was never built), Navy Pier was planned and built to serve as a mixed-purpose piece of public infrastructure. Its primary purpose was as a cargo facility for lake freighters, and warehouses were built up and down the Pier. However, the Pier was also designed to provide docking space for passenger excursion steamers, and in the pre–air conditioning era parts of the Pier, especially its outermost tip, were designed to serve as cool places for public gathering and entertainment. The Pier even had its own tram. Today, the pier is one of the most visited attractions in the entire Midwestern United States and is Chicago's number one tourist attraction.

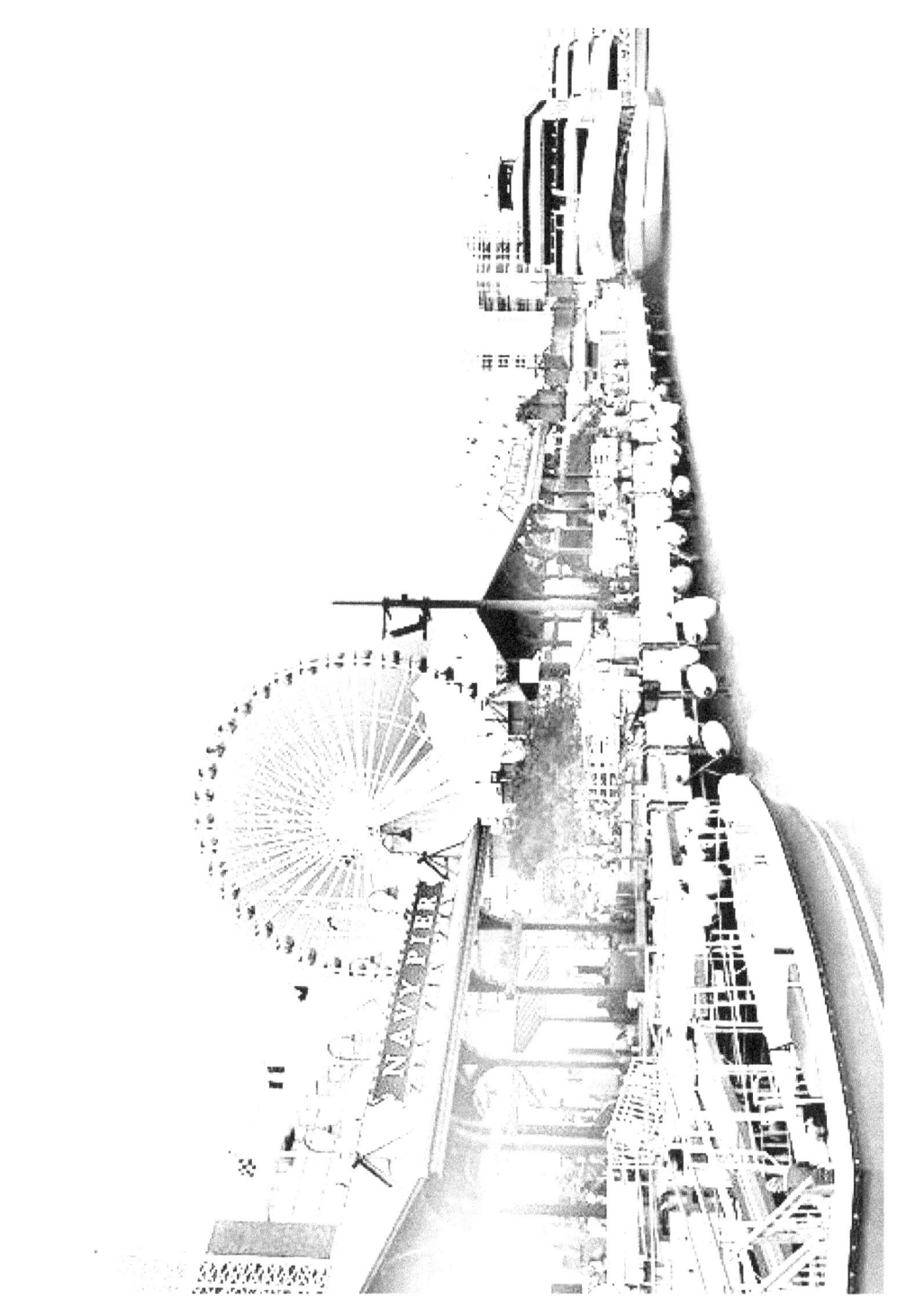

The #1 McDonald's Store

The McDonald's #1 Store Museum is housed in a replica of the former McDonald's restaurant in Des Plaines, Illinois, opened by Ray Kroc in April 1955. The company usually refers to this as The Original McDonald's, although it is not the first McDonald's restaurant but the ninth; the first was opened by Dick and Mac McDonald in San Bernardino, California, in 1940, while the oldest McDonald's still in operation is the fourth one built, in Downey, California, which opened in 1953. However, the Des Plaines restaurant marked the beginning of future CEO Kroc's involvement with the firm. It opened under the aegis of his franchising company McDonald's Systems, Inc., which became McDonald's Corporation after Kroc purchased the McDonald brothers' stake in the firm.

The actual Des Plaines restaurant was demolished in 1984, but McDonald's realized they had a history to preserve, so they built a replica. With golden arches soaring over a glass and metal, red-and-white tiled exterior, the building largely follows the McDonald brothers' original blueprints, which they had introduced when they began franchising in 1953; a Phoenix, Arizona, restaurant was the first built in this manner. Kroc's restaurant was the first McDonald's built in a colder climate, and some adaptations were made to the design, including a basement and a furnace.

The entrance sign is original, with early cartoon mascot "Speedee," representing the innovative Speedee Service System, inspired by assembly-line production, the McDonald brothers had introduced in 1948. It has, however, been moved from its original location at the south end of the property. The sign boasts "We have sold over 1 million." The replica museum offers irregular summer hours and is often closed; tours are by appointment. The ground floor exhibits original fry vats, milkshake Multimixers (which Kroc had sold when he first encountered the San Bernardino McDonald's restaurant), soda barrels, and grills, attended to by a crew of male mannequins in 1950s uniforms. Visitors can walk in through the back or peek through the order windows in front (there was no sit-down restaurant section in 1955). In the basement is a collection of vintage ads, photos, and a video about McDonald's history.

A new, modern McDonald's was built across the street, replacing a Howard Johnson's restaurant (then Ground Round). Over at the new McDonald's there are a half dozen glass-enclosed exhibits arrayed around the tables, including red and white tiles from the original restaurant and string ties worn by employees from the 1950s to the early 1970s.

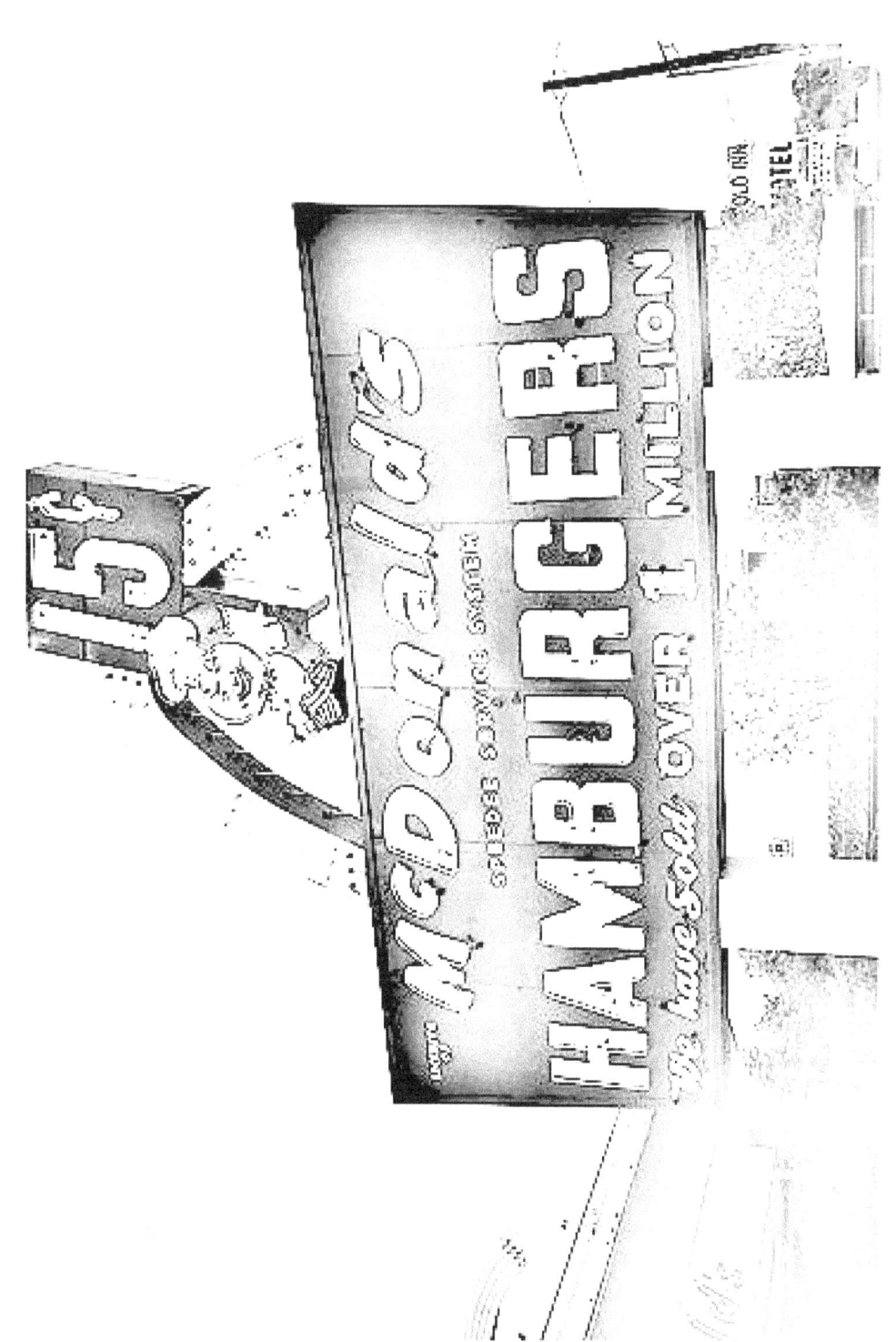

www.ingramcontent.com/pod-product-compliance
Lightning Source LLC
Chambersburg PA
CBHW080652180526
45168CB00008B/3400